"Resources made by and for people of color who are looking to grow in contemplative Christian practices are few and far between, but Made for PAX is an oasis in a spiritual desert. Their commitment to empowering and raising up voices as part of the global majority is a testament to their shalom-filled activism. The Made for PAX Bible Studies are thoughtful resources for folks who are passionate about fostering the flourishing of all."
Jenai Auman, writer and author of *Othered*

"We long for integrity—in ourselves, in society, in the church. I love how the Made for PAX Bible Studies embody integrity in both what they present and how they present it. Addressing important topics often neglected by the church, these books call us to live out a holistic faith—and do so by engaging us holistically as readers. Here are pages filled with poems, prayers, visual art, embodied practices, and more, inviting us to join Jesus, step by step, breath by breath, in the work of cultivating integrity and shalom in ourselves and in the world."
Michael Stalcup, poet

"The Made for PAX Bible Study series is a gift for anyone seeking contemplative scriptural learning. These well-structured studies offer engaging writing and thoughtfully chosen topics. The units on mental health and migration are particularly timely and important, addressing crucial contemporary issues. This is a valuable resource for those seeking deeper understanding, centering often decentered voices."
Guesnerth Josué Perea, director of Black Lives and Contemplation and the Center for Spiritual Imagination

"The Made for PAX Bible Study series is both timely and evergreen. I'm so grateful for these studies that illuminate biblical values with depth, a diversity of voices, and a commitment to peacemaking and whole-person growth."
Tasha Jun, author of *Tell Me the Dream Again: Reflections on Family, Ethnicity, and the Sacred Work of Belonging*

"Made for PAX continues to create some of the most innovative and thoughtful resources for followers of Jesus. In this powerful new work, Kristel Acevedo tackles two essential questions: What happened at the cross? And how does it impact our daily lives? With biblical depth and Christ-centered clarity, she weaves together timeless truth and practical insight, offering a fresh look at the beauty and power of the cross."
J.W. Buck, author of *Everyday Activism* and *In God's Good Image*

"*Liberated at the Cross* provides a unique invitation into the person, practice, and power of peace. Kristel Acevedo lends us her own family's story to help illuminate the greater redemption story. This study will challenge and inspire you to think about the cross differently and to embrace your calling to be a peacemaker in a chaotic world."
Dorina Lazo Gilmore-Young, Bible teacher and author of *Redeemer: God's Lovingkindness in the Book of Ruth*

LIBERATED AT THE CROSS

Peace and Reconciliation in God's Kingdom

A 6-WEEK INTERACTIVE BIBLE STUDY

KRISTEL ACEVEDO

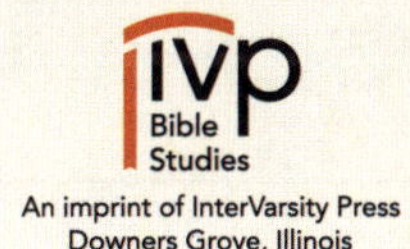

An imprint of InterVarsity Press
Downers Grove, Illinois

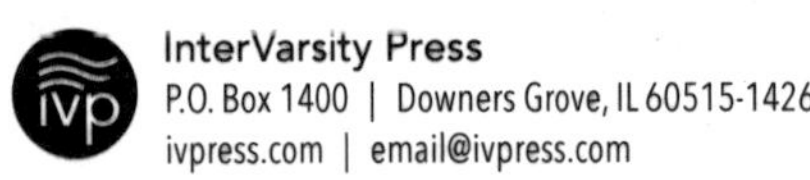

InterVarsity Press
P.O. Box 1400 | Downers Grove, IL 60515-1426
ivpress.com | email@ivpress.com

InterVarsity Press® is the publishing division of InterVarsity Christian Fellowship/USA®. For more information, visit intervarsity.org.

While any stories in this book are true, some names and identifying information may have been changed to protect the privacy of individuals.

Published in association with Joy Eggerichs Reed of Punchline Agency.

The publisher cannot verify the accuracy or functionality of website URLs used in this book beyond the date of publication.

Cover design: Faceout Studio
Cover image: © RLT_Images / DigitalVision Vectors via Getty Images
Interior design: Nat Maxey
Interior images: Made for PAX

ISBN 978-1-5140-1294-9 (print)
ISBN 978-1-5140-1295-6 (digital)

Printed in Colombia ♾

Library of Congress Cataloging-in-Publication Data
Names: Acevedo, Kristel author
Title: Liberated at the cross : peace and reconciliation in God's Kingdom : a 6-week interactive Bible study / Kristel Acevedo.
Description: Downers Grove, Illinois : IVP Bible Studies, an imprint of InterVarsity Press, [2026] | Series: Made for Pax Bible study series
Identifiers: LCCN 2025013667 (print) | LCCN 2025013668 (ebook) | ISBN 9781514012949 paperback | ISBN 9781514012956 ebook
Subjects: LCSH: Jesus Christ--Crucifixion | Bible--Study and teaching | Christian life--Biblical teaching
Classification: LCC BS680.C47 A252 2026 (print) | LCC BS680.C47 (ebook)
LC record available at https://lccn.loc.gov/2025013667
LC ebook record available at https://lccn.loc.gov/2025013668

30 29 28 27 26 25 | 8 7 6 5 4 3

CONTENTS

Liberated at the Cross

With PEACE

Do you believe the world can be changed?
Your relationships mended?
Your past addressed?
Your future improved?
Do you believe our churches can be more engaged?
Our land healed?
Our bodies protected?
Our politics reformed?

With *PEACE*, this is possible.
With the Peace of Jesus, born of the cross—
All things are being made new.

The cross is more than the method God used to save us.
The cross is also the model for Christian living.

Welcome

Welcome to this six-week study on peace and reconciliation!

In this study, we focus on one critical aspect of God's story of peace: the work of the cross. Only when we understand the meaning of the cross and how the cross influences humanity and the world can we begin to perceive God's vision for the restoration of shalom in the world. Only then can we have a fuller picture of the role that God calls us to in that restoration.

This study invites you into understanding the significance of the cross of Jesus, and how it serves as the gateway to peace. By the time you complete all six sessions, you will: (1) learn how to look to the cross for hope and power to pursue peace; (2) gain a biblical understanding of how the cross impacts your discipleship journey; and (3) learn how to apply these principles in pursuit of a cross-shaped life in your everyday contexts.

Most importantly, this study offers you a better way to pursue peace and love in your community, one marked by sacrifice, nonviolence, and liberation for all people.

How to Use this Study

Here is a bird's-eye view of our six-week study:

MEANING - What is conveyed through the cross of Jesus

Session One	Fulfillment	The cross of Jesus is where the Scriptures find their climax.
Session Two	Liberation	The cross empowers Jesus to liberate the world from the power of death, sin, and unjust systems.
Session Three	Solidarity	The cross is where Jesus fully displays the solidarity of God with those who are oppressed by the powers of empire.

METHOD - The technique by which God accomplishes peace

Session Four	Self-Giving Love	Followers of Jesus are called to embody the cross of Jesus through self-giving love.
Session Five	Nonviolent Resistance	Followers of Jesus learn from the cross that we are to resist evil and injustice in the world.
Session Six	Enemy Love	Followers of Jesus learn from the cross that we are to forgive and love our enemies as a way to break the cycle of dehumanization.

EACH SESSION

01 Session Topic: Presents an overview of the week's topic.

02 Preparation: Provides an opportunity to prepare for the study through prayer and reflection questions.

03 Manifesto–Scripture Reading: Includes a Scripture reading that serves as the manifesto statement (declaration) for the session.

04 Myth & Material–Eight to Ten Minute Video: Offers a video that covers the Myth (lies we believe) and Material (central truths) for the session.

05 Small Group Discussion: Prompts group discussion with questions. Discussion is the central part of this journey, where you have the opportunity to allow the Spirit of God to move you in the direction you should go.

06 Motion-Embodied Action: Concludes with a Motion section for you to practice throughout the following week and lead you toward more concrete embodied action.

ENGAGING THIS STUDY

Set aside a designated day and time for a weekly gathering–in person or virtually–for the next six weeks. The Introduction offers foundational thoughts and the opportunity for reflection that will frame the subsequent weeks. The session videos are accessed through the QR codes in the book. These videos were created with a group in mind–that you would watch the video together and then immediately engage in the content that follows. But individuals still have personal access to the videos, in case someone misses a group gathering. At the end of each session, participants are given prompts that encourage reflection on the session's key themes throughout the week.

Remembering the Cross

I was texting with a friend early one morning. She felt discouraged as the news of a crisis in Cuba spread across social media. And she was disappointed by the response of politicians and organizations—people she voted for and trusted to fight for the oppressed.

Due to extreme shortages of food and medicine, a series of protests against the Cuban government began in July 2021. The situation in Cuba was already dire, but the Covid-19 pandemic had made everything worse. The Cuban people were suffering.

My friend and I were both raised in Miami, Florida, the Latin American capital of the United States. Immigrants from all over the world—but especially Latin America—pour into this city. Cuba itself is only ninety miles from the coast of Florida. The streets of Miami buzz with salsa music, and the sweet nectar of *cafecito* runs through our veins. The influence of Cuban culture is evident in every corner of our city.

Who will fight for justice?

So, when our people cry out in anguish, we not only hear it, we feel it.

What could I tell my friend who was feeling hopeless and powerless in this dire situation? What could I possibly point her to when people in positions of power were failing us on all sides? Who would stand for the oppressed? Who would fight for justice? Who would speak up for those who have no voice?

I remembered the cross. The cross was a barbaric tool of torture in the ancient Roman world. It was a brutal form of execution meant to instill fear in all who witnessed the practice. Bodies were hung on wooden beams for days so that anyone who walked by would be reminded of their fate if they dared speak against the regime.

That's how dictatorships work too. Dictators rule over a country and crush anyone who speaks against them. They withhold food, medicine, and basic necessities to show how they can easily wield their power. Witnesses of the horrors and injustices are filled with fear that they could be silenced next.

The power of Jesus lives in us.

But something else happened when Jesus was crucified. Was it horrible and evil? Of course. Jesus was subjected to inconceivable physical pain, and sin and evil were poured onto Jesus' shoulders. However, Jesus remained undefeated. He resurrected. And the same power that lives in him now lives in us.

Meaning of the Cross

We look to the meaning of the cross for our power and hope in a world longing for the peace of God.

The cross is one of the most distinct symbols of Christianity. As a child, my family attended mass at our local Catholic church. Behind the altar was a crucifix. I remember wondering how on earth this—a beaten man hanging on a bloodied cross—could be an adored symbol. How could this be a picture of God's love?

To the world, the cross is foolish. Crucifixion was nothing to be celebrated in ancient times. Hanging on a cross was degrading. It meant you were a criminal. It meant you were subhuman, shamed, and tortured. It meant God had forgotten you.

When Jesus was crucified, many decided he couldn't be who he said he was. Clearly, he was a madman or a con artist. Even his disciples were confused. Had they been following a fraud this entire time? Could they have been wrong about Jesus being the Messiah?

But then the resurrection occurred. Now we know the truth of Jesus. As his disciples, we recognize that what sounded foolish to the world was God's wisdom and love for us.

> For the message about the cross is foolishness to those who are perishing, but to us who are being saved it is the power of God. For it is written,
>
> > "I will destroy the wisdom of the wise,
> > and the discernment of the discerning I will thwart."
>
> Where is the one who is wise? Where is the scholar? Where is the debater of this age? Has not God made foolish the wisdom of the world? For since, in the wisdom of God, the world did not know God through wisdom, God decided, through the foolishness of the proclamation, to save those who believe. For Jews ask for signs and Greeks desire wisdom, but we proclaim Christ crucified, a stumbling block to Jews and foolishness to gentiles. (1 Corinthians 1:18-23)

For the Christ-follower, the cross represents love, hope, joy, and peace. God's mercy for us is put on full display as Jesus willingly went to the cross to create a path back to God. Despite our own disobedience and propensity for sin, he still chooses us. He still loves us. He still frees us from sin, death, and evil. He humbled himself by becoming obedient to the point of death, a torturous death on a cross (Philippians 2:8).

The cross ushers in God's upside-down kingdom. God's kingdom isn't about being the most powerful, strongest, or best. It's about God's power showing up in our weakness and gaining victory through sacrifice. Jesus knew that on the other side of that cross would be an indescribable joy that we would share in (Hebrews 12:2). We get to be reunited with God for eternity.

The cross ushers in God's upside-down kingdom.

The cross may have been an evil tool used by the Romans, but we know that God is in the business of taking the evil of this world and using it for good. God used the cross to bring about forgiveness for our sins. He used it to rescue us from death and separation from him, and to bring the restoration of shalom.

Through this divine victory, Jesus is beginning to bring liberation from all the spiritual forces that manifest in oppression all around us. Now that we have been made righteous, we are called as followers of Jesus to live into the reality of our freedom, and to work toward making freedom a reality for all right now.

At the cross is where God begins to make all things new. And we get to join him on that mission. As followers of Christ, we too bring love, hope, joy, and peace everywhere we go. The cross is our example that shows us how we can press against the patterns of this world and follow the better way of Jesus.

Method of the Cross

The cross of Jesus provides patterns that shape the way we follow Jesus.

The cross is not simply the source of personal, social, and spiritual liberation. The cross also provides a shape for how Christians are to live, think, and act in the world. Although some people believe that the purpose of the cross is only to pardon humanity, the New Testament is clear that the cross is also the pattern we conform our lives to and live into as God's people. Thus, we look to the method of the cross as the *shape* of the Christian life.

This is called *cruciformity*.[1] New Testament scholar Michael Bird says, "The cross is not merely a tenet of faith that we are required to assent to; it is a manifesto we are to follow. Christians are not called merely to believe in the cross, but more properly to live it out."[2]

When we look at Scripture, we can identify three principles—self-giving love, nonviolent resistance, and enemy love—that provide a framework for cruciformity to promote peace in this world. As we explore these principles, we will learn what it means to be conformed to the image of Christ. We will learn how to be agents of peace in a world that doesn't understand why we would want to join Jesus on the cross. Faithfulness to the cross is rebellion against the world. It shows the world who we are, that we will continue to love people and pursue peace because that's what our God does.

Christians are called to live out the cross.

I think back to my friend and the many others who wondered how to respond to crises in Cuba. We know that, because of the cross, we are not powerless. We are powerful. We also know that the world may not recognize our power. While the world may use force or violence, we are marked by peace and love. We show a broken world a path that leads to wholeness—*shalom*.

So, how do we do that? We sacrifice our time and resources to bring awareness and relief when and where we can. We resist wrongdoing and oppression, and speak up for the oppressed. We love our enemies, which includes the oppressor, because we know that we also need the love of Jesus. We offer forgiveness to all because God does not withhold forgiveness from anyone.

The Cuban people and all who are suffering in this world are not forgotten—not by God and not by God's people.

REFLECTION QUESTIONS

01 Why have you shown up for this journey?

02 What makes you want to learn more about the cross?

03 What do you think living out the cross might look like?

SESSION ONE

Fulfillment

Fulfilln

In Session One we will explore the concept of violence and peace in our world, and how the cross of Jesus makes peace possible.

Fulfillment

Liberation

Solidarity

Self-Giving Love

Nonviolent Resistance

Enemy Love

ent

As you consider these topics, you may wonder how the violent act of crucifixion brings peace to an already violent world. It seems like a paradox. But when we stop to think about it, paradoxes are all around us.

When I gave birth to my son, it was the most painful experience I had ever had. I chose to forgo pain medication and embraced the labor process. The contractions came in fast waves; at one point, I was scared I wouldn't be able to do it. But as soon as my son made his entrance into the world and the midwife placed him on my chest, I was filled with joy—the best and most unique joy I had ever felt. From my greatest pain came my greatest joy.

In the same way, Jesus endured the greatest pain of taking on the sin of the whole world on the cross, so that we would be brought into God's diverse, vibrant, multiethnic family. As the apostle Paul wrote, "There is no longer Jew or Greek; there is no longer slave or free; there is no longer male and female, for all of you are one in Christ Jesus. And if you belong to Christ, then you are Abraham's offspring, heirs according to the promise" (Galatians 3:28-29).

Pulse Check

Share any questions or concerns you have as you begin this study.

01 What are you looking forward to learning?

02 How do you want Jesus to shape your view of violence in our world?

03 How are you hoping this study helps you to pursue peace, despite the violence you may encounter?

Preparation

To prepare for Session One, follow this grounding practice and read the accompanying prayer. Be present with those you are with, and be attentive to what God might impress upon you during this time.

We start with a grounding practice because our world is always on the go. We're often expected to show up, produce, and execute. This is a time for us to come together and consider shalom—God's dream for us to be whole, flourishing, and at peace. Shalom is God's dream for us to be fully human. This grounding practice reminds you to slow down, breathe, and invite the God of Peace to settle you before you begin the group study.

GROUNDING PRACTICE

Take Three Deep Breaths

Inhale: God of Peace ***Exhale: I Am Here***

Inhale: God of Peace ***Exhale: I Am Yours***

Inhale: God of Peace ***Exhale: I Am Ready***

Manifesto

The cross of Jesus is where the Scriptures find their fulfillment.

Isaiah 2:2-4

In days to come
the mountain of the LORD's house
shall be established as the highest of the mountains
and shall be raised above the hills;
all the nations shall stream to it.
Many peoples shall come and say,
"Come, let us go up to the mountain of the LORD,
to the house of the God of Jacob,
that he may teach us his ways
and that we may walk in his paths."
For out of Zion shall go forth instruction
and the word of the LORD from Jerusalem.
He shall judge between the nations
and shall arbitrate for many peoples;
they shall beat their swords into plowshares
and their spears into pruning hooks;
nation shall not lift up sword against nation;
neither shall they learn war any more.

When I read the Old Testament, I'm often struck by the violence contained in its pages, from Cain murdering Abel to entire cities wiped out in war. But if you look carefully, you will see an underlying theme—*una promesa*, a promise.

The ancient Scriptures spoke of someone who would come from the royal line of David[1] and usher in an age of peace for everything and everyone.[2] Called the "Prince of Peace,"[3] this person would teach the nations to reject everything that disrupts true peace.

Surprisingly, God fulfills this purpose not through conquering armies or by subjugating earth, but through the cross of Jesus:[4] "He came and proclaimed peace to you who were far off and peace to those who were near" (Ephesians 2:16-17). Through his life and death, Jesus cultivates a deep care for the earth and others.[5]

The work of the cross is where the Scriptures find their culmination. Jesus came, speaking peace on earth, but it was only through his death and resurrection that true, holistic peace was made possible.

REFLECTION QUESTIONS

01 In the story of the cross, from the Old Testament to the New Testament, what do I find strange or hard to believe?

02 What does God's plan to bring holistic peace through the cross of Jesus tell us about the character of God?

Scan the QR code to watch the Session One Myth & Material video. As you watch the video, write down any statements that stand out to you or thoughts that you have.

Myth

Peace comes from our circumstances, not from the cross.

Material

We often search everywhere for peace, until we realize it can only be found in Jesus.

DISCUSSION QUESTIONS

01 How is the cross the ultimate fulfillment of Scripture? How does that lead to peace?

02 In the past, what circumstances have you looked to for the fulfillment of peace? How has that played out in your life?

03 Where do you see a need for greater peace in your life or the lives of others today?

Benediction

When the circumstances of our lives overwhelm us,
may we be overwhelmed by the peace of Christ.
When the empires of the world try to take over,
may we be more committed to the kingdom of God on earth as it is in heaven.

When we forget that God is sovereign over all of creation,
may we be reminded that not one leaf blows in the wind without him knowing about it.

Amen.

Motion

For this week's Motion exercise, we will participate in the ancient practice of *lectio divina*. This simply means *sacred reading*. This way of reading Scripture helps us to slow down and connect to the heart of our Father in heaven.

You can do this activity on your own throughout the week. If possible, try to do it at least three times during the week before we move to Session Two.

Lectio Divina

Find a quiet spot and make yourself comfortable. You may want to dim the lights or light a candle. Create an atmosphere that will minimize distractions and help you focus. It may help to have soft music playing in the background.

Begin your time with intentional silence. Invite the Holy Spirit to quiet your heart and mind. When you are ready, you can begin reading and praying through **Philippians 2:8-11**, following the process on the next page.

He humbled himself
and became obedient to the point of death—
even death on a cross.
Therefore God exalted him even more highly
and gave him the name
that is above every other name,
so that at the name given to Jesus
every knee should bend,
in heaven and on earth and under the earth,
and every tongue should confess
that Jesus Christ is Lord,
to the glory of God the Father.

Lectio (Read)

This is your first reading of the passage. Read it slowly and prayerfully, opening yourself up to the presence of God. You may want to read silently or out loud. Notice any words or phrases that jump out at you. Trust that God will bring to mind what he wants to emphasize. Allow for a time of silence after reading the passage.

Meditatio (Reflect)

On the second prayerful reading of the passage, focus on the words or phrases that jumped out at you in the first reading. Reflect on why God would highlight these words to you. Try not to analyze the text too deeply, but rather receive what God has for you during this time. Ask him questions and listen for his response.

Oratio (Respond)

Read the passage for a third time, and then respond. This is your opportunity to respond to whatever it is the Father is inviting you to. You may find it helpful to journal your response so you can go back and read it later. You can also simply pray aloud or silently.

Contemplatio (Rest)

The focus of the fourth prayerful reading is to rest in the love God has for you. You don't have to do or say anything. Let the Holy Spirit fill and refresh you. Sit in silence as long as you need to.

Liberation

Liberat

This is the second of three weeks exploring the meaning of the cross, or what is conveyed through the cross of Jesus.

Fulfillment

Liberation

Solidarity

Self-Giving Love

Nonviolent Resistance

Enemy Love

ion

Last week we saw how the cross of Jesus was the fulfillment of God's promise to Abraham to make a family and bring about peace to all. From great violence came great joy.

This week, in Session Two, we'll dig deeper to see how the cross set the stage for the liberation of the world. Jesus set humanity free from death, sin, and evil. Once he accomplished this, he took his rightful place as King of the kingdom.

Pulse Check

In Session One's Motion section, you practiced lectio divina. Take some time to share your experience.

01 Was it your first time doing this practice?

02 Did you sense God telling you anything?

03 How can you incorporate this practice into your regular rhythms?

Preparation

To prepare for Session Two, follow this grounding practice and read the accompanying prayer. Be present with those you are with and be attentive to what God might impress upon you during this time.

We start with a grounding practice because our world is always on the go. We're often expected to show up, produce, and execute. This is a time for us to come together and consider shalom—God's dream for us to be whole, flourishing, and at peace. Shalom is God's dream for us to be fully human. This grounding practice reminds you to slow down, breathe, and invite the God of Peace to settle you before you begin the group study.

GROUNDING PRACTICE

Take Three Deep Breaths

Inhale: God of Peace ***Exhale: I Am Here***

Inhale: God of Peace ***Exhale: I Am Yours***

Inhale: God of Peace ***Exhale: I Am Ready***

Manifesto

The cross of Jesus liberates the world from the power of death, sin, and unjust systems.

Ephesians 2:12-22

Remember that you were at that time without Christ, being aliens from the commonwealth of Israel and strangers to the covenants of promise, having no hope and without God in the world. But now in Christ Jesus you who once were far off have been brought near by the blood of Christ. For he is our peace; in his flesh he has made both into one and has broken down the dividing wall, that is, the hostility between us, abolishing the law with its commandments and ordinances, that he might create in himself one new humanity in place of the two, thus making peace, and might reconcile both to God in one body through the cross, thus putting to death that hostility through it. So he came and proclaimed peace to you who were far off and peace to those who were near, for through him both of us have access in one Spirit to the Father. So then, you are no longer strangers and aliens, but you are fellow citizens with the saints and also members of the household of God, built upon the foundation of the apostles and prophets, with Christ Jesus himself as the cornerstone; in him the whole structure is joined together and grows into a holy temple in the Lord, in whom you also are built together spiritually into a dwelling place for God.

When you think of the cross, what comes to mind? Is it peace? Freedom? Victory? Perhaps the first time you saw a crucifix or read the details of the crucifixion, you did not immediately think of these things. And yet, the cross brings about the promise of peace that God made to his children.

On the cross, God overcame everything that disrupted his perfect shalom, including evil forces and systems, and the evil within the human heart.[1] He cleanses us of our unrighteousness,[2] frees us from sin,[3] and empowers us with the Holy Spirit to live a new kind of life.[4]

Even more, with unjust forces and systems defeated, the cross enables the liberation of all creation from the hatred, violence, spiritual darkness, and greed that oppress us. Today God is carrying out the work of recreating peace between all things.[5] One day, this kingdom will be fully realized.[6]

This universal, everlasting peace with God and others is possible because of the liberation of the cross. And we, as followers of Jesus, are called to live out and work toward this reality now.

REFLECTION QUESTIONS

01 According to Ephesians, how are our very identities changed by the cross?

02 What are tangible ways in which you have seen the liberation of Jesus at work in the world? In what areas has liberation not yet arrived?

Scan the QR code to watch the Session Two Myth & Material video. As you watch the video, write down any statements that stand out to you or thoughts that you have.

Myth

Liberation comes through grand acts of military takeover.

Material

Jesus, through the cross and resurrection, brings about true, lasting liberation.

DISCUSSION QUESTIONS

01 How have you thought about the concept of liberation? Are there ways in which you have experienced the true, lasting liberation of Jesus?

02 Why did Jesus choose to come as the very opposite of a military conqueror—as a poor, humble man from an oppressed people group? Why was this necessary for our liberation?

03 How does knowing that Jesus has conquered sin and death change our perspective about this life and eternity? How might it affect the way we live in a world that is still full of violence and evil?

Benediction

Jesus, King of the Universe and Liberator of All:

Help us to join you on your mission to bring freedom to this world.

Help us to have our allegiance completely and only to you.

Help us to point others to you, the only one who can bring true peace.

Amen.

Motion

For our Motion practice this week, we will reflect on a song from Chris Renzema, called "Son of God." You can listen to the song once or multiple times throughout the week.[8]

Focus on these lyrics:

> ***We have seen the greatness of our King, hope that all will be redeemed***
> ***But not by military might, but by the Man who bled and died***

Pray through these lyrics and journal about what they mean to you.

ESSION THREE

Solidarity

Solidar

This week we close out our focus on the meaning of the cross—what Jesus' crucifixion and resurrection mean for humanity and how we live—by looking at solidarity.

Fulfillment

Liberation

Solidarity

Self-Giving Love

Nonviolent Resistance

Enemy Love

ity

In Session One, we examined how Jesus' crucifixion and resurrection are the fulfillment of the Scriptures through which God's shalom is possible. In Session Two, we studied how the cross liberates the world from the power of sin, death, and evil. He is a mighty King who frees us all through the humble cross.

This week, in Session Three, we look at how the cross shows us the solidarity God has with those who are oppressed.

Pulse Check

Take a moment to check in on how you felt about last week's study.

Were you challenged in your way of thinking? If so, what has been your response to that challenge? Take your questions to God and ask the Holy Spirit to help you wrestle through them.

Preparation

To prepare for Session Three, follow this grounding practice and read the accompanying prayer. Be present with those you are with and be attentive to what God might impress upon you during this time.

We start with a grounding practice because our world is always on the go. We're often expected to show up, produce, and execute. This is a time for us to come together and consider shalom—God's dream for us to be whole, flourishing, and at peace. Shalom is God's dream for us to be fully human. This grounding practice reminds you to slow down, breathe, and invite the God of Peace to settle you before you begin the group study.

GROUNDING PRACTICE

Take Three Deep Breaths

Inhale: God of Peace ***Exhale: I Am Here***

Inhale: God of Peace ***Exhale: I Am Yours***

Inhale: God of Peace ***Exhale: I Am Ready***

Manifesto

The cross is where Jesus fully displays God's solidarity with those who are oppressed by the powers of the empire.

The cross demonstrates how God stands in solidarity with oppressed people. Jesus did not choose an easy death; he allowed himself to be killed by crucifixion,[1] the Roman Empire's punishment for those who dared to challenge their authority. The two men crucified next to Jesus were also accused of insurrection.[2] In short, Jesus was considered a rebel and suffered alongside other rebels.

Through the crucifixion, Jesus was "exalted" by God as King of Peace over the cosmos,[3] and he forever allied himself with those who are hurt by oppression and injustice. As a result, bringing the peace of God to earth will always involve liberating and empowering people who are poor, marginalized, and oppressed.[4]

Matthew 25:31-46

When the Son of Man comes in his glory and all the angels with him, then he will sit on the throne of his glory. All the nations will be gathered before him, and he will separate people one from another as a shepherd separates the sheep from the goats, and he will put the sheep at his right hand and the goats at the left. Then the king will say to those at his right hand, "Come, you who are blessed by my Father, inherit the kingdom prepared for you from the foundation of the world, for I was hungry and you gave me food, I was thirsty and you gave me something to drink, I was a stranger and you welcomed me, I was naked and you gave me clothing, I was sick and you took care of me, I was in prison and you visited me." Then the righteous will answer him, "Lord, when was it that we saw you hungry and gave you food or thirsty and gave you something to drink? And when was it that we saw you a stranger and welcomed you or naked and gave you clothing? And when was it that we saw you sick or in prison and visited you?" And the king will answer them, "Truly I tell you, just as you did it to one of the least of these brothers and sisters of mine, you did it to me." Then he will say to those at his left hand, "You who are accursed, depart from me into the eternal fire prepared for the devil and his angels, for I was hungry and you gave me no food, I was thirsty and you gave me nothing to drink, I was a stranger and you did not welcome me, naked and you did not give me clothing, sick and in prison and you did not visit me." Then they also will answer, "Lord, when was it that we saw you hungry or thirsty or a stranger or naked or sick or in prison and did not take care of you?" Then he will answer them, "Truly I tell you, just as you did not do it to one of the least of these, you did not do it to me." And these will go away into eternal punishment but the righteous into eternal life.

REFLECTION QUESTIONS

01 What specific aspects of Jesus' experience of the cross (from his arrest and trial to his execution and burial) demonstrate his solidarity with those who have been harmed by oppression and injustice? How does his solidarity affect our perspective of him as God?

02 In the parable in Matthew 25, Jesus draws a clear distinction between people who served and cared for those in need, and those who didn't. What does this passage tell us about Jesus? What does it tell us about what it means to be a disciple of Jesus?

Scan the QR code to watch the Session Three Myth & Material video. As you watch the video, write down any statements that stand out to you or thoughts that you have.

Myth

Jesus is concerned primarily with spiritual matters and doesn't get involved with earthly matters.

Material

On the cross, Jesus identifies with the vulnerable and displays God's solidarity with those who are oppressed.

DISCUSSION QUESTIONS

01 Is there a certain vulnerable or oppressed group that grabs your heart? Share with your group.

02 When has someone said "that's just the way it is" about a social injustice or challenge that you care about? How did that make you feel?

03 Name one or two tangible, practical ways that you can partner with God to usher in his kingdom and care for the oppressed around you.

Benediction

May the Lord give you eyes to see the oppressed around you.

May the Lord give you a heart that cares for the oppressed around you.

May the Lord give you wisdom, compassion, and grace for the oppressed around you.

Be empowered by his Spirit as you bring heaven to earth with him.

Amen.

Motion

For our Motion practice this week, we will do a centering prayer. This is a quick, powerful, and Spirit-filled way to regulate our body's nervous system and remember who God is.

Find a quiet spot and put your hand on your heart.

Breathe in through your nose and out through your mouth.

Think of a word you want to focus on.
In the context of our study, it could be peace *or* liberation.

Repeat this word to yourself over and over as you breathe in and out.

This will help clear your mind and refine your focus.

Use this centering prayer throughout your week as needed.

SESSION FOUR

Self-Giving Love

Self-Gi
Love _

This week, in Session Four, we will look at the method of the cross.

Fulfillment

Liberation

Solidarity

Self-Giving Love

Nonviolent Resistance

Enemy Love

ving

In the first three sessions, we focused on the meaning of the cross for us and how we live. We looked at how the cross is the fulfillment of Scripture. It liberates the world from the power of death, sin, and unjust systems. And it exemplifies Jesus' solidarity with the oppressed and marginalized.

This week, in Session Four, we will look at the method of the cross: how the cross of Jesus provides patterns that shape the way we follow him. What is the way of Jesus in our world today? It's made up of the same components that he modeled when he was on earth: self-giving love, nonviolent resistance, and enemy love toward the forces standing against the peace of God. Today, we will explore self-giving love.

Pulse Check

Share with the group about the centering prayer you practiced this past week.

If you were able to practice the centering prayer, how was the experience? What was its impact?

Preparation

To prepare for Session Four, follow this grounding practice and read the accompanying prayer. Be present with those you are with and be attentive to what God might impress upon you during this time.

We start with a grounding practice because our world is always on the go. We're often expected to show up, produce, and execute. This is a time for us to come together and consider shalom—God's dream for us to be whole, flourishing, and at peace. Shalom is God's dream for us to be fully human. This grounding practice reminds you to slow down, breathe, and invite the God of Peace to settle you before you begin the group study.

GROUNDING PRACTICE

Take Three Deep Breaths

Inhale: God of Peace ***Exhale: I Am Here***

Inhale: God of Peace ***Exhale: I Am Yours***

Inhale: God of Peace ***Exhale: I Am Ready***

Manifesto

Followers of Jesus are called to follow the pattern of the cross by practicing self-giving love.

Philippians 2:5-11

Let the same mind be in you that was in Christ Jesus,

who, though he existed in the form of God,
did not regard equality with God
as something to be grasped,
but emptied himself,
taking the form of a slave,
assuming human likeness.
And being found in appearance as a human,
he humbled himself
and became obedient to the point of death—
even death on a cross.

Therefore God exalted him even more highly
and gave him the name
that is above every other name,
so that at the name given to Jesus
every knee should bend,
in heaven and on earth and under the earth,
and every tongue should confess
that Jesus Christ is Lord,
to the glory of God the Father.

Jesus chose to die on the cross because he is obedient to God's deep love,[1] a love that seeks to reach out and reconcile even when—especially when—that love is not returned. We know from Scripture that salvation is only possible through voluntary self-emptying and self-humbling,[2] a giving of one's entire self to pursue peace.

We see this from Jesus when, just before his arrest, he prays, "Not my will but yours be done" (Luke 22:42). Jesus, Son of God, sovereign over all creation, willingly submits himself to the torture, torment, and death of the cross. He does not resist or fight with words or actions, even knowing that this will cost him his very life.[3] This is how much he trusts God and God's loving plan of salvation.[4]

We are called to this same way of life. As followers of Jesus, we are called to live with self-giving love toward the world.[5]

REFLECTION QUESTIONS

01 What words or phrases in the Philippians passage and the text above most capture your attention? Why?

02 When you consider following Jesus' self-giving path, what is your immediate response? Does it seem possible?

Scan the QR code to watch the Session Four Myth & Material video. As you watch the video, write down any statements that stand out to you or thoughts that you have.

Myth

If you live with self-giving love, you will not have enough for yourself.

Material

As followers of Jesus, we live in an upside-down kingdom that promotes self-sacrifice over self-preservation.

DISCUSSION QUESTIONS

01 Is there someone you know who has modeled self-giving love? Share about that person with your group.

02 How is God inviting you to be self-giving? What are some specific ways in your daily life? Write them down.

03 Why is it important to remember that it's only through our union with Christ that we are able to fulfill the call to be self-giving?

Benediction

May you empty yourself, as Jesus emptied himself.

May you humble yourself and become obedient to God, as Jesus humbled himself and became obedient to God, even to death on the cross.

May you take on the mind and attitude of Christ, because you belong to him.

Amen.

Motion

There are many different types of prayer. One of them is the prayer of consecration. This is a prayer in which we set ourselves apart to follow God's will. An example of this is when Jesus prayed, "My Father, if it is possible, let this cup pass from me, yet not what I want but what you want" (Matthew 26:39).

In the first couple of days after completing this session, take some time to write your own prayer of consecration. Reflect on these questions to help you shape your prayer:

01 What does God set his people apart for?

02 What has God set you apart for?

03 How does this affect your heart, mind, body, and soul?

As you pray, make a conscious and willing decision to dedicate all of yourself to God.

Recite your prayer once a day until the next meeting.

Nonviolent Resistance

Nonvio
Resista

In Session Five, we will discuss nonviolent resistance. When we live cross-shaped lives, we actively resist the evil of this world, but we don't use violence to do it.

Fulfillment

Liberation

Solidarity

Self-Giving Love

Nonviolent Resistance

Enemy Love

lent
nce

We're nearing the end of this study. We spent the first three sessions examining the meaning of the cross, exploring its fulfillment of Scripture, the liberation it enables, and how the cross is an expression of God's solidarity with the vulnerable and oppressed.

In the previous session, we transitioned to examining the method of the cross. We looked at the self-giving nature of Jesus on the cross as an example of how we should sacrificially live. Instead of living from a scarcity mentality, we can remember and trust in the abundance found in Christ. We can choose self-sacrifice over self-preservation.

Pulse Check

Take a moment to share the prayer of consecration you created in the past week.

01 How did your perspective change as a result of reading this prayer daily?

02 After sharing your prayers, discuss examples of how you were able to choose self-sacrifice over self-preservation in the past week.

Preparation

To prepare for Session Five, follow this grounding practice and read the accompanying prayer. Be present with those you are with and be attentive to what God might impress upon you during this time.

We start with a grounding practice because our world is always on the go. We're often expected to show up, produce, and execute. This is a time for us to come together and consider shalom—God's dream for us to be whole, flourishing, and at peace. Shalom is God's dream for us to be fully human. This grounding practice reminds you to slow down, breathe, and invite the God of Peace to settle you before you begin the group study.

GROUNDING PRACTICE

Take Three Deep Breaths

Inhale: God of Peace ***Exhale: I Am Here***

Inhale: God of Peace ***Exhale: I Am Yours***

Inhale: God of Peace ***Exhale: I Am Ready***

Manifesto

The cross teaches us to resist evil and injustice in the world.

When Jesus begins his ministry, he declares that the gospel is for those in need of salvation, liberation, forgiveness, and healing.[1] His words and actions focus on blessing the disadvantaged, marginalized, and oppressed. In doing so, he pushes against the social, religious, and political status quo.[2] Each of Jesus' intentionally subversive acts builds up to and culminates in his death on the cross—the greatest act of willful nonviolent resistance against evil and injustice.[3]

Webster's Dictionary defines *resistance* as an "effort made to stop or to fight against someone or something; an opposing force." The word *force* has three definitions. The first two speak to physical strength or power, violence used on a person or thing. The third definition, however, is "strength or power that is not physical"—in other words, *nonviolent*. This is the type of resistance Jesus exerted throughout his ministry on earth and on the cross.

As followers of Jesus who are called to the way of the cross, we also are invited into the practice of nonviolent resistance. The way of Jesus includes ongoing resistance to the spiritual, physical, and social oppression we see around us. We do this with our prayer, our bodies, our activism, and our very lives.

Luke 4:16-22

When he came to Nazareth, where he had been brought up, he went to the synagogue on the Sabbath day, as was his custom. He stood up to read, and the scroll of the prophet Isaiah was given to him. He unrolled the scroll and found the place where it was written:

"The Spirit of the Lord is upon me,
because he has anointed me
to bring good news to the poor.
He has sent me to proclaim release to the captives
and recovery of sight to the blind,
to set free those who are oppressed,
to proclaim the year of the Lord's favor."

And he rolled up the scroll, gave it back to the attendant, and sat down. The eyes of all in the synagogue were fixed on him. Then he began to say to them, "Today this scripture has been fulfilled in your hearing." All spoke well of him and were amazed at the gracious words that came from his mouth. They said, "Is this not Joseph's son?"

REFLECTION QUESTIONS

01 How do we see Jesus resisting evil and injustice during his time on earth? At the cross?

02 The cross teaches us that nonviolence and resistance go together. In what way do they go together, and what does that mean for disciples of Jesus?

Scan the QR code to watch the Session Five Myth & Material video. As you watch the video, write down any statements that stand out to you or thoughts that you have.

Myth

The only form of resistance that will work against a violent oppressor is violent resistance.

Material

The way of Jesus includes ongoing resistance to spiritual, physical, and social oppression.

DISCUSSION QUESTIONS

01 What are some powerful stories of nonviolent resistance you can recall? Share with the group.

02 What is the problem with responding to violence with violence?

03 What are some concrete examples of being a peacemaker versus a peacekeeper? What steps can you take this week toward peacemaking?

Benediction

May you follow the steps of Jesus toward peacemaking.

May you allow the Holy Spirit to empower you in peacemaking.

May you look to God in the midst of the chaos of this world.

Help us, Father, to walk in the way of nonviolent resistance.

Amen.

Motion

For this week's Motion activity, scan the QR code and take time to read this abridged version of Dr. Martin Luther King's "Letter from Birmingham Jail" at least once. It may take you fifteen to thirty minutes to read through the letter and complete the exercise below.

Notice the four basic steps Martin Luther King outlines for a nonviolent campaign:

01 Collection of the facts to determine whether injustices are alive

02 Negotiation

03 Self-purification

04 Direct action

Take some time to reflect on and journal about the following questions:

01 How did Martin Luther King carefully go through these steps in Birmingham?

02 How can you commit to these practical steps in your own life?

ESSION SIX

Enemy Love

Enemy

Welcome to the final session of this study on living a cross-shaped life!

Fulfillment
Liberation
Solidarity
Self-Giving Love
Nonviolent Resistance
Enemy Love

Love

In previous sessions, we've talked about how the cross was the ultimate fulfillment of Scripture. The cross provides liberation from and solidarity against the unjust powers and systems of our world. We've also looked at the method of the cross: how the cross provides us with a clear example of self-giving love and nonviolent resistance. We can be peacemakers in our world without giving in to the violence and chaos that surround us. Instead, we follow the example of Christ on the cross.

In our final session together, we will discuss the last principle of a cross-shaped life: enemy love. This is not something we hear about often in our world. People are not readily reaching out to their enemies with the goal of love and forgiveness. Reconciliation seems like a lost art. Through the cross, however, Jesus shows us that love and forgiveness break the cycle of dehumanization and lead to love for all, including our enemies.

Pulse Check

Think back through the various sessions. Take time to share with one another and thank God for his movement throughout these sessions.

01 Which sessions have impacted you the most? Which ones have you found the most challenging?

02 How has your perspective of peace changed? How might you want to live differently?

Preparation

To prepare for Session Six, follow this grounding practice and read the accompanying prayer. Be present with those you are with and be attentive to what God might impress upon you during this time.

We start with a grounding practice because our world is always on the go. We're often expected to show up, produce, and execute. This is a time for us to come together and consider shalom—God's dream for us to be whole, flourishing, and at peace. Shalom is God's dream for us to be fully human. This grounding practice reminds you to slow down, breathe, and invite the God of Peace to settle you before you begin the group study.

GROUNDING PRACTICE

Take Three Deep Breaths

Inhale: God of Peace ***Exhale: I Am Here***

Inhale: God of Peace ***Exhale: I Am Yours***

Inhale: God of Peace ***Exhale: I Am Ready***

Manifesto

Through the cross, Jesus teaches us to love our enemies, both near and far.

Matthew 5:38-48

You have heard that it was said, "An eye for an eye and a tooth for a tooth." But I say to you: Do not resist an evildoer. But if anyone strikes you on the right cheek, turn the other also, and if anyone wants to sue you and take your shirt, give your coat as well, and if anyone forces you to go one mile, go also the second mile. Give to the one who asks of you, and do not refuse anyone who wants to borrow from you.

You have heard that it was said, "You shall love your neighbor and hate your enemy." But I say to you: Love your enemies and pray for those who persecute you, so that you may be children of your Father in heaven, for he makes his sun rise on the evil and on the good and sends rain on the righteous and on the unrighteous. For if you love those who love you, what reward do you have? Do not even the tax collectors do the same? And if you greet only your brothers and sisters, what more are you doing than others? Do not even the gentiles do the same? Be perfect, therefore, as your heavenly Father is perfect.

Those who choose love and forgiveness are often seen as fools, asking to be taken advantage of over and over. But was Jesus a fool? After all, he preached and practiced enemy love in his life and his death.[1]

In the Sermon on the Mount, Jesus shocks those in the crowd—primarily Jewish peasants—by teaching them to love their oppressors, to carry their enemy's packs an extra mile, and to turn the other cheek.[2] Jesus lives out this teaching up to the moment of his death, forgiving those who mocked him, tortured him, and even forced him to carry his own cross.[3]

As the Son of God, Jesus could have easily called down fire onto his enemies, but he chooses forgiveness and reconciling love instead.[4] He chooses to disrupt the cycle of dehumanization, violence, and hatred, and to see his persecutors as image-bearers of God. We see in Scripture that the early church also follows this path of enemy love.[5] Today, we who follow Jesus are asked to do the same.

REFLECTION QUESTIONS

01 What is most jarring to you about Jesus' teachings in Matthew 5:38-48? How does this differ from the advice we're given or practices we see in the world?

02 What are the truths we need to believe before we can pursue and sustain love for our enemies?

Scan the QR code to watch the Session Six Myth & Material video. As you watch the video, write down any statements that stand out to you or thoughts that you have.

Myth

Our enemies don't deserve our love or forgiveness.

Material

As followers of Jesus, we can choose grace that leads to forgiveness and love, and breaks the cycle of dehumanization.

DISCUSSION QUESTIONS

01 Have you ever experienced radical forgiveness after committing a wrong? How did that feel? Does it help you extend forgiveness to others?

02 Think about a time when you or someone you know was able to practice enemy love. What did that require?

03 The *imago Dei*, or the image of God, is inherent in all of us. How does this truth change how you view others, friends or enemies? How can you honor the imago Dei in those around you?

Benediction

May you allow the grace of God to overflow from you into your areas of influence.

May you remember the example of Jesus on the cross of forgiveness and enemy love.

May you take this experience and allow it to transform your view of God, yourself, and others.

Motion

Parting Prayer

As we end our journey together in this last session, may you look back on the past several weeks and remember the foundational aspects of living a cross-shaped life. The cross is the ultimate fulfillment of all of Scripture. Through it, we find our liberation and have solidarity with our Savior King, and we see the perfect example of self-giving love, nonviolent resistance, and enemy love. The cross shows us how to live and empowers us to do so. The cross is why we have hope for a world of peace, love, and justice. Go in peace.

Take the following prayer with you as a way to commemorate our time together.

God of Peace,

We come before you with gratitude.
Gratitude for the words we read.
Gratitude for the conversations we had.
Gratitude for the sacrifice of your Son, Jesus.
Gratitude for the new life we get to walk in.
Gratitude for the peace that is ours in Christ.
Gratitude for the cross and all it represents.

As we go on in our lives,
May we remember these words.
May we remember these conversations.
May we remember the sacrifice of your Son, Jesus.
May we remember to walk in new life.
May we remember to embrace the peace that is ours in Christ.
May we remember the cross and all it represents.

Amen.

NOTES

Introduction

[1]Michael Gorman, *Cruciformity: Paul's Narrative Spirituality of the Cross* (Grand Rapids, MI: Eerdmans, 2001).
[2]Michael Bird, *What Christians Ought to Believe* (Grand Rapids, MI: Zondervan, 2016), 135.

Session One: Fulfillment

[1]2 Samuel 7:12-16.
[2]Isaiah 11:1-10.
[3]Isaiah 9:6.
[4]Ephesians 2:14-18.
[5]Isaiah 2:2-4.

Session Two: Liberation

[1]Colossians 2:15; Ephesians 1:20-23.
[2]1 John 1:9; 1 Corinthians 6:11.
[3]Romans 6:7.
[4]Romans 6:9-10.
[5]Colossians 1:20; 2 Corinthians 5:19.
[6]Isaiah 9; Daniel 2:44; 7:13-14, 27.
[7]Ephesians 2:12-22.
[8]"Chris Renzema - Son of God (Official Audio Video)," uploaded by Chris Renzema, May 31, 2019, www.youtube.com/watch?v=bbljRGc35mE.

Session Three: Solidarity

[1]Philippians 2:8.
[2]Matthew 27:38.
[3]John 3:14; 8:28; 12:32, 34.
[4]Luke 1:46-55; 4:18-19.

Session Four: Self-Giving Love

[1]Philippians 2:8.
[2]Philippians 2:7-8.
[3]Matthew 26:52-53; John 18:11, 36.
[4]1 Peter 2:23.
[5]Philippians 2:5-11; 1 Peter 2:21; 4:19.

Session Five: Nonviolent Resistance

[1]Luke 4:18-20.
[2]Luke 8:1-3, 19-21; 14:26-33.
[3]Colossians 2:15; Hebrews 12:2.

Session Six: Enemy Love

[1]Matthew 5:38-48; Luke 6:35-36.
[2]Matthew 5:41.
[3]Luke 23:24, 34.
[4]Romans 5:6-11.
[5]Romans 12:9-21; 1 Peter 2:18-25.

Made for PAX provides faith resources by Christians of color and empowers Christians of color through the PAX Fellowship, a nine-month program serving contemplatives, creatives, community builders, and church leaders at the intersection of peace, justice, and contemplation.

To learn more, visit ***www.madeforpax.org***.

 *facebook.com/madeforpax*

 *instagram.com/madeforpax*

 *linkedin.com/company/madeforpax*